PRESENTED TO

Cejae Sánchez

FROM

Katie Waswick & Lauren Reed

DATE

May 20, 2006

Nothing can separate you from the love of God.
Thank you for being the wonderful person God created.

TEACUPS
FULL OF
TREASURES

Let the Names of God
Be Your Source of Strength

mary grace birkhead

Design by Brand Navigation
Bill Chiaravalle, DeAnna Pierce,
Russ McIntosh & Brittany Gerwig

INTEGRITY®
PUBLISHERS
Nashville

THIS BOOK IS DEDICATED TO MY GRANDMOTHER,

EMMA JEAN DANIEL,

WHO POURS GOD'S TRUTH

AND HER LOVE INTO MY LIFE. I LOVE YOU.

Thank you to my husband, Rob, who is my Boaz. To my sweet children, Robert, Daniel, and Camille, who point me back to Christ. Thanks also to the people who love me enough to ask the hard questions: Virginia Bousquet, Renee Draughon, Jodie Theilen, Doyle Yarbrough, Susan Lipson, Julie Ward, Melinda Seibert, Debbie Crenshaw, Carol Virden, and my pastors, Lloyd Shadrach and Jeff Schulte. To the brave people at Integrity Publishers for believing in these books: Byron Williamson, Mark Gilroy, Barb James, Betty Woodmancy, Dale Wilstermann, and Joey Paul. And special thanks to Bill Chiaravalle, DeAnna Pierce, Russ McIntosh, and Brittany Gerwig for making this book so beautiful.

INTRODUCTION

My grandmother collects teacups. Her cabinets are filled with them—all sizes, shapes, and colors. Each teacup represents a special memory. When we have tea together, she lets me choose the teacups. Part of our time together is spent talking about the ones I have chosen. I love to hear the stories. Our time together gives me greater perspective and helps me see life's bigger picture. My grandmother, Emma Jean Daniel, pours beautiful truth into my life.

The Bible, like my grandmother's cabinet, is filled with beautiful treasures. Among them are the many names of God.

Each name reveals a part of His character. Learning His attributes and meditating on their meanings allows us to know Him more intimately.

This book takes the names of God from both the Old Testament and the New Testament. The Old Testament references come from the original Hebrew and Aramaic translations. English versions of the Bible usually refer to God as simply "God" or "Lord" and do not reflect the specific significance of the name. For example, "Jehovah Rophe" means "God as healer," but is referred to in English translations simply as "Lord." This is unfortunate, because each original name gives a deeper look into His true nature. The New Testament references are the attributes of God's character that will give you deeper insight into who He is.

Accept each page of this book as a treasure from Him. As you reflect on the scripture passages, He will reveal himself to you. When you apply the specific meaning of His name in each scripture, it will give you great hope and bring light and life to your current circumstances. He is kind and loving and longs for you to know Him better. So relax, have a cup of tea, and treasure these moments with Him.

~ OLD ~
TESTAMENT

YAHWEH

PSALM 19:14

God is your Redeemer.

You can't mess up so badly

that He can't make it all work out.

He can fix anything!

He can take your past mistakes and

make them treasures.

YAHWEH JIREH

GENESIS 22:14

God is your Provider.

You can trust that

He will supply all that you need.

It's all His anyway!

Remain open.

Lift your needs to Him and

allow Him to provide in His way.

JEHOVAH - NISSI

EXODUS 17:15

God is your Banner.

This is your new identity: You are His!

You are no longer a victim. You're a victor!

You don't have to be defeated

by your circumstances;

He's in there fighting for you!

YAHWEH SHALOM

JUDGES 6:24

God is your Peace.

He can bring rest to your soul.

He wants to tie up all the loose ends!

Peace can be found, not in controlling,

but in knowing who is in control

of all things.

JEHOVAH - ROPHE

EXODUS 15:22-26

God is your Healer.

You can be whole—in mind, body and spirit!

He is the Great Physician!

He created you and can bring

order to your chaos.

JEHOVAH - ROHI

PSALM 23

God is your Shepherd.

You are cared for,

tended to, and watched over.

You are His!

He seeks you when you wander away

and draws you back to Him.

JEHOVAH-TSIDKENU

JEREMIAH 23:5

God is your Righteousness.

You don't have to work for His approval.

If you trust Him for your salvation,

He has declared you innocent and accepted!

It's not about what you can do for Him;

it's about what He has already done for you.

EL ROI

GENESIS 16:13

God opens your eyes.

He sees all things;

nothing escapes His mighty gaze.

Through Him you can see beyond

your circumstances.

He wants you to see the bigger picture

of your life!

KANNA

EXODUS 20:5

God is jealous for you.

You are His bride.

Let your thoughts go to Him often.

He wants the best of your attention!

You are His beloved.

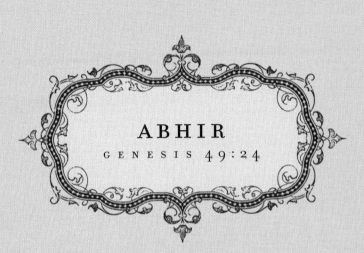

ABHIR

GENESIS 49:24

God is your Mighty One.

You are not left to fight alone.

You have His awesome power

available to you.

He protects you with His mighty hand.

He's your all-time, number one hero!

MAGEN

PSALMS 3:3, 18:30

God is your Shield.

You are guarded on every side.

He is actively at work defending you!

You don't have to become weary

protecting yourself.

You can hide in the safety He brings.

EL-OLAM

GENESIS 21:33

God is Everlasting.

He never gets old or tired!
He is the same God today as He was
thousands of years ago.
Amazingly, He knows your name!
You can enjoy Him now and forever.

ZUR

DEUTERONOMY 32:18

God is your Rock.

In an unsure world,

you can have a firm place to stand.

When life swirls around you,

making you feel insecure and confused,

God offers confidence and peace.

EL SHADDAI

GENESIS 49:25

God is more than enough.

He is completely nourishing and satisfying.
You can rest knowing He will meet your
spiritual, emotional, and physical needs.
He is your constant sustainer.

EYALUTH

PSALM 22:19

God is your Strong Tower.

You can run to Him and He will protect you.

Don't fight alone and unprotected.

God is your defender and longs

to keep you safe.

NEW
TESTAMENT

ANCHOR

HEBREWS 6:19

God is your Anchor.

Choppy waters are inevitable.

You are tethered to One who

created all things.

Don't focus on the waves; focus on His loving,

strong hands that are protecting you

in the storm.

LIGHT

JOHN 1:6-9

God is your Light.

You don't have to be afraid.

He extinguishes the dark with His light!

Replace your fearful thoughts with the

truth of who He is.

He is the One who overcomes the darkness.

ADVOCATE

1 JOHN 2:1

God is your Advocate.

You don't have to defend yourself.

Rest and know that He's taking up for you!

Turn your anxious

and fearful thoughts to Him.

He will reveal the truth in His time.

Trust Him.

BREAD OF LIFE

JOHN 6:32

God is your Bread of Life.

You can be full and not crave what

the world has to offer.

He wants to satisfy all your longings.

He has water for your thirsty soul.

Let Him sustain you with His eternal truth.

CORNERSTONE

EPHESIANS 2:20-22

God is your Cornerstone.

You are becoming a dwelling place
of the Spirit.

He is your unshakable foundation.

Lay everything at His feet.

He is the bedrock for all your life!

He is faithful.

DAYSPRING

LUKE 1:78

God is your Dayspring.

You can be revived moment by moment.

He is refreshing, invigorating, and satisfying!

Open your neediness up to Him.

Experience the mystery of Living Water

flowing through you.

DOOR

JOHN 10:7

God is your Door.

You open your life up to eternity

when you trust Him.

He is the way to heaven!

The door is open.

Enter in. Be fully known and

fully loved.

FORERUNNER

HEBREWS 6:20

God is your Forerunner.

You don't have to worry about what's ahead.

He goes out before you.

Don't be anxious about the day.

He is in front of you and beside you.

He follows behind to protect you.

VINE

JOHN 15:5

God is your Vine.

You can produce much fruit

when your source is the Vine.

He provides all you need to be successful!

On your own you are limited,

but He can lavish

you with riches from His vast storehouse.

TEACHER

LUKE 12:12

God is your Teacher.

He is the Author of all truth.

Listen to His voice and not the voices

of the world.

He will open your mind and give you clarity.

He will bless you with an unwavering spirit.

GARDENER

JOHN 15:1-2

God is your Gardener.

You will be watered, fertilized, and pruned

according to His perfect schedule.

Your power is limited. God's is unlimited!

Trust Him to use you and provide

all that you need.

He'll have you blooming in no time!

LORD

L U K E 12:31

God is your Lord.

You serve the Creator of the Universe.

He is worthy of your efforts and praises!

He sees all your hard work and is

pleased that your heart wants to bless others.

You are precious to Him and

He delights in you.